NATURAL WORLD

POLAR BEAR

HABITATS • LIFE CYCLES • FOOD CHAINS • THREATS

Malcolm Penny

WAYLAND

WWF

Produced in Association with WWF-UK

NATURAL WORLD

Chimpanzee • Elephant • Giant Panda • Great White Shark
Killer Whale • Lion • Polar Bear • Tiger

Produced for Wayland Publishers Limited by
Roger Coote Publishing
Gissing's Farm, Fressingfield
Suffolk IP21 5SH, UK

First published in 1999 by
Wayland Publishers Limited
61 Western Road, Hove
East Sussex BN3 1JD, England

All Wayland books encourage children to read and help them improve their literacy.

✓ The contents page, page numbers, headings and index help locate specific pieces of information.

✓ The glossary reinforces alphabetic knowledge and extends vocabulary.

✓ The further information section suggests other books dealing with the same subject.

find Wayland on the Internet at http://www.wayland.co.uk

Cover: Eye-to-eye with a polar bear.
Title page: A bear peers out from woods in Cape Churchill, Canada.
Contents page: Stretching up to get a better view.
Index page: Bears enjoy a playful roll in the snow.

WWF is a registered charity no. 201707
WWF-UK, Panda House, Weyside Park
Godalming, Surrey GU7 1XR

British Library Cataloguing in Publication Data
Penny, Malcolm
  Polar bear: habitats, life cycles, food chains, threats. -
(Natural world)
  1.Polar bear - Juvenile literature
  I.Title
  599.7'86

ISBN 0 7502 2447 9

Picture acknowledgements
Bruce Coleman Collection 6-7 (Mr Johnny Johnson), 7 (Joe McDonald), 14 (Mr Johnny Johnson), 15 (Fred Bruemmer), 18 (Staffan Widstrand), 20 (Tom Schandy), 23 (Fred Bruemmer), 28 (Mr Johnny Johnson), 29 (Staffan Widstrand), 31 (Mr Johnny Johnson), 34 (Mr Johnny Johnson), 35 (Staffan Widstrand), 36 (Fred Bruemmer), 39 (Staffan Widstrand), 41 (Fred Bruemmer), 44m (Mr Johnny Johnson), 45t (Staffan Widstrand), 45m (Mr Johnny Johnson), 45b (Staffan Widstrand), 48 (Fred Bruemmer); Bryan and Cherry Alexander 1, 3, 8, 12, 13, 16, 17, 21, 25, 26, 27, 30, 33t, 37, 38, 42, 43; Digital Vision 40; Oxford Scientific Films 9 (Norbert Rosing), 10 (Norbert Rosing), 11 (Norbert Rosing), 44t (Norbert Rosing); Still Pictures 22-3 (Philippe Henry), 24 (Klein/Hubert), 32-3 (Joel Bennett), 44b (Philippe Henry); Tony Stone Images *front cover*. Artwork by Michael Posen.

Contents

Meet the Polar Bear

The polar bear is the largest carnivore living on land. It lives in the freezing cold climate of the Arctic, close to the sea or on the sea ice. Its thick white coat acts as camouflage in the snow, as well as keeping it warm.

Coat
The fur looks white because it reflects light from the snow. The hairs are actually transparent and hollow. They are waterproof and trap air to keep the bear warm and dry.

An adult ▶ polar bear.

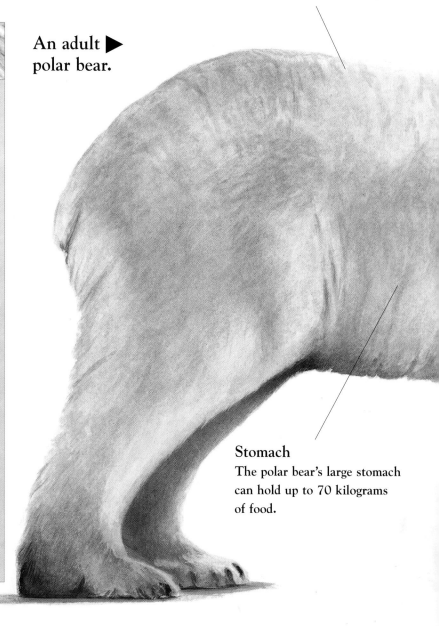

POLAR BEAR FACTS

The polar bear's Latin name, *Ursus maritimus*, means 'sea bear'.

●

A polar bear can run at 50 kilometres per hour on land or ice, but only for short distances.

●

The biggest polar bear ever recorded, in Alaska in 1960, measured 3.39 metres from nose to tail (the length of a small car) and weighed 1,002 kilograms.

Stomach
The polar bear's large stomach can hold up to 70 kilograms of food.

The red and brown shading on ▶ this map shows where polar bears live in the wild. The red areas are land, and the brown shading shows areas where the sea freezes over to form ice.

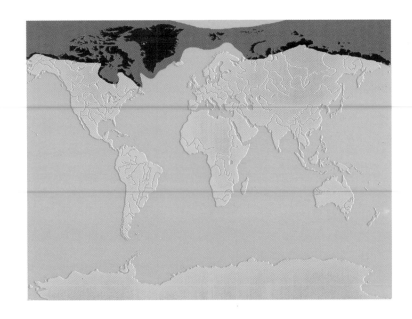

Skin

The polar bear's skin is black. This helps keep it warm because black absorbs more heat than any other colour. Under the skin is a thick layer of fat, or blubber.

Ears

A polar bear's ears are small, so that they lose less heat.

Eyes

A polar bear has no eye-lashes (they would collect ice), but it has a third eyelid, called a nictitating membrane, to protect its eyes against bright light.

Nose

A polar bear has a very good sense of smell. It can smell a dead whale from 30 kilometres away.

Feet

The soles of a polar bear's feet are covered in fur, so that it can move silently without slipping on the ice. Its claws are very sharp, to grip its prey. The bear's toes are partially webbed to help it swim.

The World of the Polar Bear

Polar bears live all round the Arctic, wherever there is ice on the sea. Although they spend most of their time on the ice, they are excellent swimmers. They can swim for hundreds of kilometres from one ice floe to the next. Their waterproof coat and thick layer of fat enable them to float easily. They can also dive underwater for as long as two minutes.

▼ Polar bears gather on a frozen lake in Manitoba, Canada.

► A brown bear
emerges from
hibernation in
north-west USA.

The polar bear's closest relations are European brown bears, and American brown bears and black bears, which live in North America.

Its other relations live in tropical forests. They are the Asian black bear, which lives from Iran to Japan, the sun bear of Southeast Asia, the spectacled bear from western South America and the sloth bear, which lives in eastern India and Sri Lanka.

7

A Polar Bear is Born

Polar bears mate in April or June, and the females are pregnant for six and a half to nine months. In November, a pregnant female polar bear digs a den, usually in a snow drift. At the end of a passage 2–6 metres long, she makes a chamber where she will stay until spring comes. Some females use the same den year after year.

▼ A female polar bear roams the edge of the ice on the coast of Svalbard, Norway.

Although female polar bears stay in their dens for four or five months, they do not really hibernate. Their heart slows from 70 to about 8 beats per minute, but their temperature and breathing stay near normal. Animals that do hibernate can take several days to wake up, but a dozing polar bear can wake in an instant.

▲ The entrance to a female polar bear's breeding den. This is where she gives birth to her young and keeps them warm through the winter.

9

Birth

The cubs are born about six weeks after the female enters her den. There are usually two cubs. Sometimes there is only one, and very rarely three or even four. The newborn cubs are tiny – about the size of rats – and they weigh 600–700 grams. They are blind and deaf, and completely helpless.

▲ These twin cubs are only about ten weeks old.

Although it is warmer in the den than outside, the temperature still falls below freezing. The mother keeps her cubs warm by cuddling them in her arms and by breathing on them. She feeds them with her milk, which is very high in fat. The mother does not feed at all. She lives off the fat she has stored in her body during the summer.

▼ Newborn cubs drink milk from their mother's four teats as often as they can.

POLAR BEAR CUBS

Polar bear cubs open their eyes when they are about thirty-three days old. They start to hear after twenty-six days.

•

The cubs stay in the den with their mother until March, when they weigh 8–12 kilograms.

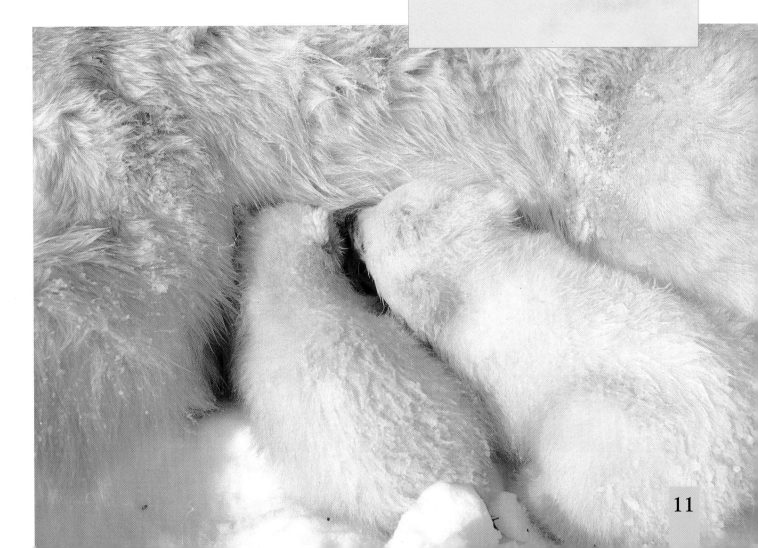

Into the White World

By March or early April, the cubs have grown to about the size of small dogs. The male cubs are already slightly larger than the females. The chamber at the end of the tunnel starts to get quite crowded. The cubs are quite happy where they are, feeding off their mother's milk. But their mother is beginning to feel hungry.

▼ A young cub plays with its mother, shortly after coming out of the den.

Finally, the mother breaks out of the den, pushing the snow away and poking her head into the air above. She must watch out for male bears, which might kill her cubs so that she would be ready to mate again. When the mother is sure that there is no danger, she climbs out on to the snow, and the cubs follow her.

When the cubs first see the huge white world outside their den, they play and slide in the snow, rolling and tumbling with their mother. They will return to the den for a week or more to sleep, but now the open Arctic wilderness is their home.

▲ A polar bear family relaxes in the great white wilderness.

13

Walking to the Coast

The cubs are still feeding on their mother's milk, but her stores of fat are almost used up. She has gone five months without food and she is thin and very hungry. If she does not feed soon she won't be able to produce enough milk for her cubs. She has to take them to the coast, where she knows she can find food.

▲ The cubs usually follow their mother in a line, but if the snow is very deep and soft, they run alongside her so they don't fall into her deep footprints.

The family might have to walk 20 kilometres to the hunting grounds. The mother bear could walk all the way in one journey, but her cubs are too small and weak to travel all day and all night. She stops every few hours to feed them and give them a chance to rest. All the time she watches out for male bears.

▼ While the young cubs sleep, their mother keeps watch.

Protecting the Young

Female polar bears take very good care of their cubs, and defend them against any danger. They usually keep well clear of adult male bears, but if one threatens her family, a mother can drive off a much larger male.

There are two reasons for this. The first is that she is very fierce when defending her cubs. The second reason is that a male dare not risk getting injured in a fight. If he cannot hunt, he will starve to death.

▼ This mother has driven off an attacking male, but her cub has been badly injured.

16

▲ An alert mother sniffs the breeze for the scent of danger. She always stays alert to protect her cubs.

If there is not much food available for a long time, hungry mother bears have been known to kill their cubs and eat them, in spite of their natural instincts to protect them. Young, inexperienced mothers sometimes do the same. The mother's instinct to survive is stronger than her instinct to protect.

MOTHER BEARS

Polar bear mothers have been known to rear up and leap at helicopters carrying research scientists, to defend their cubs from the noisy intruder.

●

If a mother polar bear loses her cubs, she will sometimes adopt others. One tagged female was found with a different set of cubs from those that she had with her a few months previously.

Hunting for Food

Polar bears feed mainly on seals. Ringed seals are their favourite, followed by bearded seals. They catch harp and hooded seals as well, and sometimes scavenge on dead walruses and whales.

▲ A cub waits patiently for food while its mother watches for a seal to come up for air.

When she has cubs with her, a mother catches adult seals for herself, and young ones for her cubs. The cubs lie quietly on the ice while she hunts, waiting for her to bring their food. When they are older, they will follow her, gradually learning to find food for themselves.

The best place for a polar bear to find its prey is at a hole in the ice, where seals come up for air. The bear can tell by the smell whether a hole is in use. It stands perfectly still by the hole until a seal appears, and then knocks it out with a single blow of its paw. A polar bear can lift a seal weighing 250 kilograms out of the water with its jaws.

▼ The polar bear's food chain depends on a steady supply of the tiny swimming animals known as plankton.

POLAR BEAR FOOD CHAIN

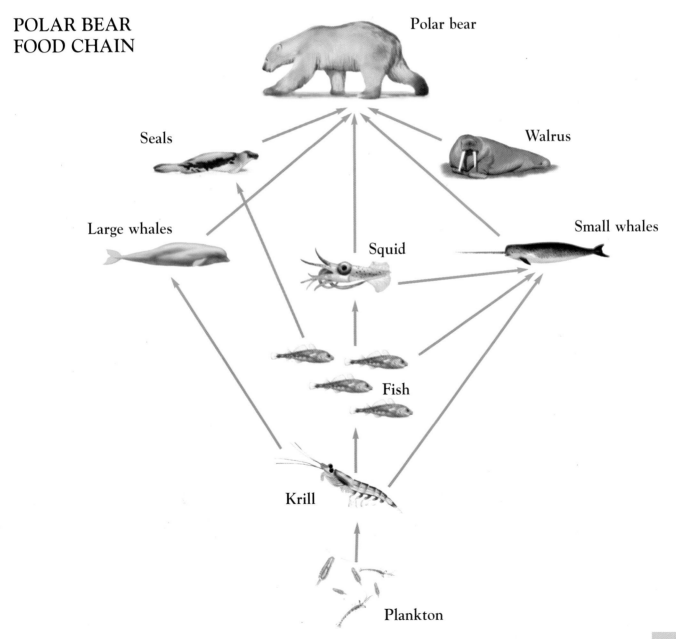

Polar bear

Seals

Walrus

Large whales

Squid

Small whales

Fish

Krill

Plankton

Stalking

As well as lying in wait, polar bears also stalk seals on the ice. They often catch hooded seals and harp seals as they bask on the ice. The bear creeps across the ice on its belly, using ridges and hummocks to hide behind until it is within about 20 metres – close enough to charge.

▼ Polar bears don't usually eat all that they kill. The left-overs are an important source of food for ivory gulls and Arctic foxes, which follow bears wherever they go. You can see the gulls in this photo, waiting to have their share of the food.

EATING

Polar bears are very clean animals. After feeding on a kill, they wash themselves carefully in water or snow.

●

When a polar bear kills a seal, it eats only the intestines and the blubber under the skin.

► Once it has left its mother's lair, a young ringed seal has a better chance of escaping hungry polar bears.

In April and May, the bears hunt young ringed seals in their lairs under the snow. The mother seal digs the lair before her pup is born. The snow melts and re-freezes around her, forming a hard crust of ice. When a polar bear sniffs out the lair, it jumps repeatedly on the ice with its front feet until the roof breaks. The seal pup has no chance of escape.

▲ Polar bears are excellent at swimming and diving. They can swim silently under water, holding their breath, as they look out for prey.

Other Foods

Polar bears eat other food besides seals. They kill small whales, such as narwhals and belugas, when they find them trapped in narrow leads in the ice. A group of bears in the Bering Sea once killed forty belugas and dragged them out on to the ice to eat.

Polar bears sometimes eat seaweed on the beach. At first, people thought it was because the bears were starving. But then they saw them diving to collect seaweed in winter, when there was plenty of other food available. The seaweed contains vitamins that the bears may need to keep healthy.

In Canada's Hudson Bay, polar bears have been seen hunting ducks. They swim quietly underwater beneath a flock of ducks dabbling at the surface, and then bob up to grab them from below.

▼ These two polar bear cubs are digging out seaweed from under the snow.

Feeding in Summer

In summer, the ice melts and seals are harder to catch. Polar bears have to find other sources of food. They might patrol the beaches below seabird colonies, looking for fallen eggs and chicks. Sometimes they steal the eggs of eider ducks, which make their nests on the ground.

▼ Summer can be a hungry time for a polar bear. This bear is looking for food along the coast.

▲ An eider duck sits tight on her nest, relying on her camouflage to hide from polar bears and other predators.

Polar bears also hunt lemmings. They dig them out of their burrows or catch them on the surface. They also dig in the soil to find grass roots and plant tubers.

In a bad summer, a polar bear may have nothing to eat for weeks. Young cubs depend on their mother for milk all this time, but if she cannot find enough food, the whole family might die.

A mother polar bear suckles her cubs until they are at least twenty months old. In places where the climate is especially cold, she may look after them for another year.

When the cubs are weaned, the mother is ready to mate again and the cubs are driven away. They have to set out on their own and hunt for themselves. They will only survive if they have learnt how to hunt well from their mother. Many cubs starve to death after leaving home.

▲ In driving snow, these two-year old cubs need their mother if they are to survive.

▶ A mother bear waits for a seal to surface. She can smell its breath from the last time it surfaced.

Leaving Home

After leaving home, young bears spend most of their time on their own. They explore their new surroundings and learn to hunt. They do their best to avoid adult males, who would kill them. Only about four out of ten young bears survive their first winter. Most of the rest starve to death.

▲ Thin ice makes travelling difficult for a young bear, alone in the frozen world.

▼ The size of a polar bear's range depends on how much food it contains. Where food is scarce, a single bear may roam an area of more than 200,000 square kilometres.

Polar bears were once thought to wander the Arctic, travelling wherever they wanted. But scientists now think that each bear has its own home range. A young bear might travel more than 1,000 kilometres to set up a home range away from its mother. Home ranges often overlap, but they are usually so large that there is little chance of a young bear meeting another of its kind.

Meeting and Greeting

When polar bears do meet, it is usually at a large supply of food such as a dead whale. To avoid fights, they have a special way of greeting one another. The two bears circle each other, grunting quietly, until they touch noses. They often begin sparring, to see which is the strongest. The weaker of the two soon realizes it would be dangerous to start a fight.

Although they are silent when they are alone, polar bears have a wide range of signals to tell others how they feel. They use a variety of grunts and growls, with angry hisses and threatening roars if they are injured.

▶ Young bears wrestle in play. At this age, they have nothing to fear from polar bear cubs of their own size.

▼ Two adult bears meet on the shore of Hudson Bay in Canada. After approaching each other cautiously, they touch noses in greeting.

Bears at the Dump

The most crowded population of polar bears in North America is around Hudson Bay, where between 100 and 150 cubs emerge from their dens each spring. When the sea-ice melts in summer, they are joined by other bears until hundreds of them spread out across the landscape looking for food.

▼ Bear cubs forage in the town dump at Churchill, Manitoba, in Canada. They are fearless and curious, but they may get ill from eating garbage.

POLAR BEARS AND PEOPLE

The tourist trade in Churchill, the 'polar bear capital of world', is worth between two and three million dollars a year.

●

Polar bears can be playful as well as fierce. When one climbed aboard a Canadian coastguard vessel, the crew tried to drive it away with a powerful hose. But the bear enjoyed the shower, raising its front legs to let the water flow under its armpits.

Many bears gather to feed at the town rubbish dump in Churchill, Manitoba. Scavenging among the smouldering piles of rubbish, the bears get scorched and filthy, so they are continually going to the sea to wash. Because they are so tame and easy to approach, Churchill is a favourite place to watch bears. The town has developed a thriving tourist industry based on the bears.

▲ Inquisitive bears make great photo-opportunities for tourists.

A Fully Grown Bear

Females usually have their first cubs when they are five or six years old. After that, they breed every three or four years until they are about twenty-one. Males are mature at three years, but few of them mate successfully until they are at least six.

◀ This adult bear stands over 3 metres tall.

ADULT POLAR BEARS

Male polar bears reach full size at eight to ten years old, and females at five or six. Both males and females can live to about thirty years old.

A fully grown male measures 2–2.5 metres from nose to tail, and weighs 300–800 kilograms. Adult females reach 1.8–2 metres, and weigh 150–300 kilograms.

▲ Longing to get back to its hunting grounds on the ice, a bear pants in the warm autumn sunshine.

Polar bears migrate with the seasons, always staying within reach of the edge of the ice. As the ice grows southwards in winter, they move south. In summer, when the ice melts again, the bears are forced northwards. Only pregnant females and their cubs live in dens throughout the winter. Other adults spend most of the winter roaming the ice.

Keeping Warm

Winter temperatures in the Arctic can be −50 °C for days or weeks on end. Polar bears survive this bitter cold easily because their bodies are so well-insulated. Their thick coat traps warm air next to the skin, and under the skin is a layer of blubber up to 11 centimetres thick.

In fiercely cold winds, a polar bear may dig out a shelter in a snow bank. Then it curls up and waits for the wind to die down.

▲ A polar bear shelters from a storm in a hole it has dug in a bank of loose snow.

▼ This polar bear is running across the ice. Polar bears rely on stealth, not speed, to catch their prey.

Polar bears lose very little body heat, even in the coldest weather. In fact, they are more likely to get too hot than too cold, especially if they move too fast. This explains why polar bears usually walk quite slowly and rarely run very far.

The Mating Season

Polar bears mate in late March to mid-May. Mature males can smell a female that is ready to mate from far away, and they will follow the scent until they find her. After mating, the male leaves.

If a male finds a female, he may kill her cubs, which will cause her to come into season so that he can mate with her.

During the mating season, rival males often challenge each other in disputes over females. Each fluffs out his coat to make himself look as big as possible. Males often swagger along, growling, to emphasise their size and weight. Polar bear researchers call this the 'cowboy walk'.

▶ With his coat fluffed out, a male bear performs the 'cowboy walk' to scare off his rivals.

◀ The air is full of signals for a male polar bear, with his finely-tuned sense of smell.

Threats

An adult polar bear's only enemies are humans and, on rare occasions, other bears. The most serious threats caused by humans are the spread of oil and gas industries, pollution by toxic chemicals and the effect of climate change. These all affect the polar bear's habitat.

▼ Offshore oil rigs can pollute the sea, threatening marine life not only in the Arctic, but also throughout the world.

THREATS TO OTHER BEARS

Hunting, poaching and habitat loss are the three main threats to other species of bears.

•

Bear hunting is allowed by the governments of some countries, to control the numbers in areas where there are too many bears.

•

Illegal poaching takes place by hunters, who sell body parts such as heads, furs or paws for high prices.

•

Habitat loss happens as human populations continue to grow and move into bear territories. The small bears that live in the tropics are threatened because the forests where they live are being cut down for timber, and to create new farmland.

▲ Scientists take samples to check the level of pollution in a polar bear's blood. The bear has been put to sleep by a dart fired from a gun.

Drilling for oil and gas can cause pollution, which harms both polar bears and the animals they hunt for food. Toxic chemicals, which are carried to the Arctic by the wind from industrial areas, can cause the same harm.

Global warming is causing some of the Arctic ice to melt, which means the polar bears' habitat is getting smaller.

▶ This polar bear skin is being dried on a frame outside a house in north-western Greenland.

◀ Native peoples are allowed to hunt polar bears for their own use. The Inuit around Thule in Greenland kill about 100 a year to make boots and trousers for the winter.

Protecting Polar Bears

Inuit have hunted polar bears for thousands of years. Traditional hunting with spears did not harm the population as much as modern rifles do. Inuit are still allowed to kill some bears each year, mainly for their skin. A polar bear's skin is warm and waterproof – ideal for Arctic clothing.

Until the International Agreement on the Conservation of Polar Bears and their Habitat in 1973, hundreds of bears were killed each year by commercial hunters, who sold the skins. Hunting for sport or for money has now almost ceased. In the 1950s there were only about 5,000 polar bears. Today there are around 40,000, but it is difficult to count them accurately because they are so scattered.

You will find a list of wildlife organizations helping to protect polar bears on page 47.

Polar Bear Life Cycle

 **1** Between one and four cubs (usually two) are born in their mother's den in December. She feeds them with milk. Their eyes open after thirty-three days.

 **2** In March, the cubs emerge from the den to follow their mother to the coast where she hunts for seals.

 **3** The cubs lie quietly in the snow while their mother goes to find food for herself, to keep up her supply of milk.

 **4** The cubs spend their first winter with their mother. In their second year, they learn to hunt, though they are still being suckled by their mother.

 **5** After leaving their mothers, polar bears spend most of their time on their own. When they do meet others, they often play with each other.

 **6** Females have their first cubs at five years old, but most males do not breed until they are six or eight. Both males and females can live to about thirty years old.

SCIENCE
- Adaptation
- Life cycles
- Food chains and webs.
- Predator/prey relationships.
- Habitat
- Materials, freezing and insulation

P.E.
- Movement, games and gymnastics on the theme 'Travelling'.

ENGLISH
- Literacy – information retrieval skills.
- Writing newspaper articles, for example human encounters with polar bears.
- Letters to conservation groups expressing a point of view.

Polar Bear Topic Web

MATHS
- Negative numbers
- Measurement, estimation of distance and weight.
- Reading scales

DESIGN AND TECHNOLOGY
- Developing a polar display.

MUSIC
- Composition

GEOGRAPHY
- Climate
- Polar Regions
- Human effects on the environment.

ART
- Work on the theme of snow and ice.
- Model making.

Extension Activities

Science
• Ask children to think about camouflage and predict and test which colours are best in the local environment. This could be carried out on the school field or in a park using small strips of coloured wool. Which colours are hardest to find?

• Gather information from the book to show how different types of bears have adapted to suit their habitats.

English
• Write leaflets and advertising literature informing people about polar bears and the area where they live.

• Debate the issue of drilling for oil in the Arctic. One group could represent an oil company, and the other could represent tourists on a polar bear-watching holiday.

Geography
• Find out about the polar region as a habitat, who else lives there and environmental threats.

Glossary

Blubber A layer of fat under the skin.
Camouflage A way of keeping out of sight by looking like the surroundings.
Carnivore A meat-eating animal.
Global warming The gradual warming of the Earth's climate caused by pollution.
Hibernate To sleep through the winter.
Home range The area where an individual animal lives and hunts.
Ice floe A vast area of frozen sea.
Insulated Protected from the cold.
Inuit Native people of the Arctic regions of North America, Greenland, and Russia.
Krill Small, shrimp-like creatures.
Lair A covered hole in the snow where a ringed seal gives birth to her pups.
Leads Clear water between ice floes.
Migrate Move from one place to another in search of food or warmer weather.
Plankton Microscopic plants and animals.
Prey An animal that is killed and eaten by another animal.
Scavenge To feed on dead animals, often those killed by a predator.
Sparring Fighting for practice or for fun.
Stalk To creep up on prey.
Suckle An animal suckles when it feeds on its mother's milk.
Toxic Poisonous.
Tubers The parts of a plant stem where it stores food underground, like a potato.
Tundra An open, treeless area in the Arctic.
Weaned Beginning to eat solid food rather than living on milk.

Further Information

Organizations to Contact

WWF-UK
Panda House, Weyside Park
Godalming, Surrey GU7 1XR
Tel: 01483 426444
Web site: www.wwf-uk.org

Care for the Wild International
1 Ashfolds, Horsham Road,
Rusper, West Sussex RH12 4QX
Tel: 01293 871596
Web site:
www.careforthewild.org.uk

Web Sites

The Bear Den
www.nature-net.com/bears/polar.html
This site has information and pictures of polar bears, and links to sites about other bears.

Polar Bears Alive
www.polarbearsalive.org/
Facts, news and pictures. This site is run by a non-profit organization dedicated to preserving the Arctic environment.

Books to Read

Animals in Hot and Cold Places by Malcolm Penny (Wayland, 1994)
Arctic and Antarctic by Barbara Taylor (Dorling Kindersley Eyewitness Guides, 1995)
Atlas of Endangered Animals by Steve Pollock (Belitha Press, 1994)
Polar Bear by Lucy Baker (Watts, 1990)
The Polar Seas by Malcolm Penny (Wayland, 1996)

Index

All the numbers in **bold** refer to photographs or illustrations.